SCHLOSS WURZACH

✳ ✳ ✳

A JERSEY CHILD INTERNED BY HITLER – GLORIA'S STORY

SUSAN SYMONS

Published by Roseland Books
The Old Rectory, St Just-in-Roseland, Truro, Cornwall, TR2 5JD

ISBN 13: 978-0-9928014-8-9
ISBN 10: 0992801486

For Gloria Bullen (born Webber), who as a child was deported from Jersey on the orders of Hitler and spent part of her childhood interned in the schloss at Bad Wurzach in the south of Germany.

CONTENTS

1

INTRODUCTION

At two o'clock in the early hours of the morning of Wednesday 16 September 1942, there was a knock on the door of ten-year-old Gloria Webber's home in Jersey. The caller was a local official and had come to deliver bad news. Her entire family, parents and five young children, were on a list of Jersey residents to be deported by the German occupying forces. The deportation order was effective immediately and they had to be at St Helier harbour, ready to leave, by four o'clock that same afternoon. Gloria and her siblings, with hundreds of other Jersey children, would lose the next years of their childhood interned on the orders of Hitler in an old castle in the south of Germany, called Schloss Wurzach.

Some seventy years later, in 2012, I retired and moved into the village in Cornwall where Gloria now lives. When we met for the first time soon after at a local event, I mentioned I was writing a book about German castles under the title of *Schloss: The Fascinating Royal History of German Castles*. To my astonishment, she responded that she had spent part of World War II shut away in such a schloss. I knew from my research that some German castles had been used as prisoner-of-war camps (the most famous example being Colditz), but

1. Child internees: this snapshot was taken in April 1945 shortly after Schloss Wurzach was liberated. Gloria is second right in the back row.

I was unaware they had also housed civilian detainees, and I had never heard of the Jersey deportations. This short book has been written with Gloria's help and is based on her recollections and her personal archive. The other sources consulted are listed on page 31, including the excellent book by author Gisela Rothenhäusler from Bad Wurzach called *Reaching across the Barbed Wire*.

This book is illustrated with Gloria's photos and some of the paintings done by her father during their detention. A map at the back shows the location of Wurzach and other key places mentioned in the book.

What is a schloss?

Schloss is the German word for castle or palace, and you are never far from one of these in Germany. For most of its history Germany was not a single, unified, country, but a patchwork of different independent states, held together under the banner of the Holy Roman Empire. The count, dukes, and princes who ruled these states were passionate builders and have left a marvellous legacy, right up until the present day, of hundreds of beautiful castles and palaces that cover the German countryside.

2

DEPORTATION
FROM JERSEY

Jersey is the largest of the Channel Islands, and is situated off the
coast of Normandy in Northern France. The island is a British
Crown Dependency and has a special relationship with the UK dating
back to the Norman invasion of 1066. Jersey is self-governing, but
shares the same monarch as the UK, and the UK is responsible for its
defence. During World War II however, its location meant that after
the fall of France it could not be defended. The Germans invaded and
occupied the island in June 1940.

The order to deport Jersey islanders came directly from Hitler, as
a reprisal for the internment by Britain of German nationals in Persia
(now Iran) in 1941. He ordered that all male residents between the ages
of sixteen and seventy who had not been born in Jersey were to be
deported to Germany, together with their families. The order was lost
for many months in a bureaucratic muddle, but had to be carried out
immediately when it came back to the Führer's notice. The bailiff of
Jersey (who is the civic head of the island and appointed by the British
crown) was informed by the German commandant on the afternoon of

2. Behind barbed wire; Wurzach internment camp painted by
Gloria's father, Thomas Webber.

15 September, just twenty-four hours in advance of the event. Despite
their reluctance to collaborate with the Germans, the bailiff and the
twelve Jersey constables (the constables or *connétables* are the elected
heads of the twelve parishes of Jersey) worked throughout these
remaining hours to inform and help those selected for deportation. It
was their local constable who knocked at the Webber's door. Gloria's
father was not a Jersey islander by birth and this is why the family were
chosen. He was originally a cockney (from East London) and met his
wife Elsie when his regiment, the East Surrey's, was stationed in Jersey.
In total the names of more than twelve hundred Jersey islanders –
men, women and children – were on the list.

The news came as a complete shock to the island. Events moved
so fast that no one was clear about who would go and who would not.
Many English-born girls were married to their Jersey-born boyfriends
that day (and the other way around) in an attempt to stay together. A
dreadful rumour circulated that the deportees were being deliberately
sent to an area of heavy allied bombing. The deportations were a
traumatic event for Jersey, both for the deportees and for their fellow

islanders left behind. For fear of hostile demonstrations, the Germans banned any public access to St Helier harbour to see them off.

Gloria still remembers this awful time in September 1942. The stress and pressure on her parents was enormous. The deportees were given only hours to arrange their affairs, deposit valuables at the bank, close up their homes, organise what few possessions to take with them, and sell or give away the rest. Many had to decide the fate of family pets. Some families made the decision to leave children behind with relatives or friends. The Webber family would stay together throughout their ordeal. As well as Gloria, aged ten, there were four younger children; her sisters Shirley, Sandra and Benita (Ben) and her brother Barry. Another sister, Angela, would be born in captivity in Germany. The Webbers had no idea where they were going or what might happen. Deportees were allowed to take only what they could carry and were instructed to bring a small suitcase; one blanket, bowl, knife, fork and spoon; and no more than the equivalent of one Jersey pound in cash.

3. Schloss Wurzach in the German federal state of Baden-Württemberg as it looks today (photo Andreas Praefcke).

4. Thomas Webber's poster, painted soon after the family arrived at Wurzach, lists the places they travelled through on their journey from Jersey.

The process of embarkation was somewhat chaotic, hampered by lack of ships, poor weather and hostile crowds. All the deportees were supposed to leave on 16 September, but in the event many did not go until nearly two weeks later. The Webber family were sent home, after hours of waiting, and told to come back in a few days. Gloria says they were unlucky when they did eventually board the ship and leave in the last group on 29 September. Because the family had small children, an over-helpful nurse pushed them to the front of the queue. There was not room for everyone on board and, when the ship sailed, those at the back of the queue were left behind. These lucky few were told to go home and avoided deportation altogether.

The boat from St Helier took the islanders to nearby St Malo on the coast of Brittany in France, where they were transferred to railway carriages and issued with provisions to last them for the journey. A 1942 painting (see illustration 4) by Gloria's father, Thomas Webber, records the names of the towns they travelled through as the train trundled across France and Luxembourg and into Germany. You can follow their route on the map on page 29. The train went south to Rennes (the capital of Brittany), where it turned east; then on through Le Mans, Paris, Rheims, Luxembourg, and across the German border. From Trier the route was south-east, past Stuttgart and Ulm until, on their third day on the train, it arrived at the small town of Biberach in the far south of Germany, more than eight hundred miles away from their homes in Jersey. Here the internees were taken off the train and walked the short distance to their first internment camp.

The camp at Biberach was a converted army barracks that had previously been used as a prisoner-of-war camp between 1940 and 1942. Called Oflag V-B, Biberach was a camp for captured officers.

5. Biberach camp by Thomas Webber; the family were held here before being sent to Schloss Wurzach.

Twenty-six British officers escaped from here in September 1941 through a tunnel. When Gloria was in the camp it was dirty, overcrowded, and entirely unsuitable for civilian internees. After a few weeks at Biberach the group of internees was split and moved again. The single men were sent to the prisoner-of-war camp at Schloss Laufen in the far east of Germany on the Austrian border, and the families went twenty miles further south to a sub-branch of the Biberach camp in the schloss at Wurzach. Gloria and her family were among nearly six hundred Channel Islanders, one hundred and eighty-six men and four hundred and eleven women and children, who arrived at Schloss Wurzach on 31 October 1942.

3

INTERNMENT
IN SCHLOSS WURZACH

The internees were horrified by what they found in Wurzach. Although the schloss might once have been grand, it was now cold, damp, in poor condition, and very dirty. The first weeks in Wurzach were extremely difficult. No arrangements had been made to accommodate women and children; conditions were basic and sanitation inadequate. There were rats in some rooms.

Without cleaning materials or equipment, internees tried to tackle the dirt by scrubbing the floors with half bricks and scraping the tables with broken glass. Winter began and temperatures plummeted. It was much, much, colder in Wurzach than in the temperate Channel Islands and the internees did not have warm clothing. There was not enough to eat and many lost weight. In December things improved a little, when warmer clothes were sent from Jersey and the first Red Cross parcels began to arrive with tins of meat, butter, biscuits and fruit, and (very popular in those days) cigarettes. But conditions were always spartan and food sparse. Gloria remembers how a loaf of bread had to last the family for five days.

Schloss Wurzach

Schloss Wurzach was a grand baroque palace built in the 1720s by Graf (Count) Ernst Jakob of Waldburg-Zeil-Wurzach. His little principality had been created in 1675 on a division of the family lands of the House of Waldburg. In the eighteenth-century, the rulers of the German states competed to show off their wealth and power through the magnificence of their palaces, and Schloss Wurzach was part of a grand plan (never realised) to transform the entire town of Wurzach into a palace complex in imitation of King Louis XIV's Versailles. The highlight of the schloss at Wurzach was the grand ceremonial staircase in the centre of the main wing, with twin staircases (one on each side) rising through the building to a colourful ceiling painting of Hercules and the gods of Mount Olympus. The Jersey internees called this staircase Marble Arch and it was the meeting place for their young people. Today it has been restored and is a wedding venue.

The independent state of Waldburg-Zeil-Wurzach existed until 1806 when it was absorbed into the larger kingdom of Württemberg as part of the shakeup of the smaller states in the Holy Roman Empire during the Napoleonic Wars. The ex-ruling family continued to own the schloss until the line of Waldburg-Zeil-Wurzach died out in 1902, when the last Graf, Eberhard, died without a male heir. The schloss became surplus to requirements as a noble residence and the buildings were sold off. Parts were used as a peat works and a brewery. The schloss was neglected and fell into disrepair; by the 1920s ivy and other vegetation was growing right up through the roof.

In 1922, Schloss Wurzach was purchased by the Catholic Order of Salvatorians, to set up a catholic seminary or boarding school. The buildings were renovated and the school opened in 1924. Over the next few years it flourished and expanded, but when the Nazis came to power and took control of the education system, its days were numbered. Subject to increasingly restrictive regulation, it eventually had to close. In 1941 the schloss was commandeered for use as a prisoner-of-war camp and housed French prisoners-of-war before Gloria's group arrived.

The Red Cross parcels were a life-line for the internees throughout their years of incarceration. Everything was used and even the packaging was salvaged. The string could be made into rope-sandals and the cellophane around the cigarette packets was folded to make belts, handbags, or brooches.

6. Elsie Webber and her six young children lived in this room in Schloss Wurzach for two and a half years.

Gloria's family adjusted as best they could to life in internment in Schloss Wurzach. The group soon organised itself, appointing a camp captain, allocating roles, and arranging rotas. Men and women lived in separate accommodation – the men in one set of communal dormitories, and the women and children in another. Mothers with several children were given a room of their own and Gloria's mother, Elsie Webber, had a small room on the first floor at the end of one side wing of the schloss. We can see this room in a painting by Gloria's father (see illustration 6), with its bare boards, single cupboard, and washing hanging from a string on the wall. Thomas Webber lived with the other men but was allowed to spend time with his family. In later years he wrote notes on the back of some of his paintings from Schloss Wurzach. 'It wasn't as clean as this ...' he wrote on the back of that of his wife's room.

Gloria lived in this room for two and a half years with her mother, her three younger sisters and her younger brother. A fourth sister, Angela, was born in the small hospital in Wurzach in October 1943; one of five babies born to the internees. Elsie Webber always said she was grateful that her children had been young during their confinement, because this meant they were resilient and did not really understand what was happening to them. In those days it was considered to be the woman's job to care for children and inevitably the biggest burden fell on Elsie, who had the herculean task of keeping six young children fed, clothed, clean, healthy and happily occupied, when everything was scarce and with absolutely no modern conveniences. As the eldest daughter, Gloria spent a lot of her time trying to help her mother and looking after her sisters and brother. She feels the worst legacy for her of these years is that she missed out on much of her education. Schooling in

7. So near, yet so far away – the view out through the barbed wire from Elsie Webber's room.

the camp was irregular and considerably hampered by lack of teaching materials. The only lesson Gloria remembers with clarity is learning to sew with Mrs Peacock (a fellow internee). When they eventually returned to Jersey, Gloria was so pleased to get back to school!

The internees had to contend with boredom, lack of privacy, and the tensions of life in confinement. Barbed wire surrounded the schloss and there was hardly any outdoor space in the camp compound for children to play or adults to exercise. After a time weekly walks outside the

8. Gloria on the elaborate staircase of Schloss Wurzach in 2005. It was known to the internees as *Marble Arch*.

camp were permitted, in crocodile formation and under guard. As a chance to stretch their legs and see the surroundings, these walks were popular. The internees were not officially permitted any contact with the people of Wurzach who were forbidden to talk to them. But the walks were nevertheless an opportunity to encounter the locals and, if the guard turned a blind eye, to barter. Red Cross tins and cigarettes were exchanged for vegetables and other fresh produce. The German children envied the child internees who, courtesy of the Red Cross, occasionally enjoyed a piece of chocolate or a biscuit! Such luxuries had disappeared in Germany. Gloria remembers how on Christmas Eve the internees gathered on the staircase of the schloss and a young Jersey boy, who had a good singing voice, sang the carol *Silent Night* (which was originally written in German). Later the German guards told them that the towns people had also listened from outside the gates.

When he came out of the army, Gloria's father became a painter and decorator by trade. While he was interned at Schloss Wurzach,

Thomas Webber discovered that he was also a talented artist. He painted pictures that are both a record of camp life and vivid works of art. Some of his paintings from these years survive. In one of these (illustration 7) we see the view from the window of his wife's room, of a street in the small town of Wurzach. It looks so normal, with a bakery, bank, and hairdresser, and it is just yards away; but it was the other side of the barbed wire and so in a different world to the internees. The same

9. Thomas Webber's powerful New Year's card for 1944 shows how the internees yearned for freedom.

10. The side wing of Schloss Wurzach which housed Elsie Webber's room.

view appears in his picture entitled *Souvenir of Wurzach Internment Camp Germany, Christmas 1942* (illustration 4). This also includes the list of places the internees travelled through on their route from St Helier. The figures of Justice (often blindfold) and Time became a trademark of his work. The figure of Time appears in a powerful picture he painted as a New Year's Greetings card for 1944 (illustration 9). Father Time stands in front of a window: through this we can see green pastures and a new dawn coming up over a village on the distant hillside. Above the rising sun is the word Freedom.

Thomas was one of a group of artists who painted during their internment in Schloss Wurzach. Their paints came from the Red Cross parcels, but paper was always in short supply and sometimes non-existent. To extend their range of subjects, the artists swapped cigarettes from the Red Cross parcels with their guards in return for postcards, and painted local scenes from these. The organised walks outside the schloss also provided them with inspiration. One of Thomas Webber's most picturesque works of art is a Wurzach landscape with the

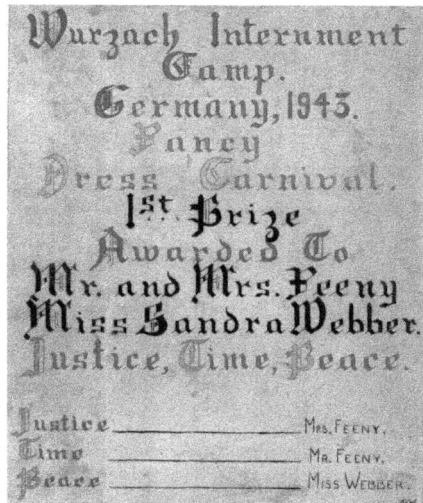

11. Prize certificate for a camp event by Thomas Webber.

river flowing between two rows of houses (see illustration 12). Built out from the river banks are wooden platforms where the local women used to do their washing. The artists also made birthday and other greetings cards, and posters for events organised by the internees. A prize certificate, painted by Thomas, shows that first prize in the fancy dress carnival in 1945 was won by the entry called Justice, Time, and Peace. One of his daughter's, Sandra, played the role of Peace.

4

LIBERATION
AND REPATRIATION

Wurzach civilian internment camp was liberated by Free French troops on 28 April 1945. The last weeks of their captivity were as difficult for the internees as the first. With the Allies advancing across mainland Europe, and the Germans in retreat, transport was in chaos. The Red Cross parcels did not get through on a regular basis and food shortages increased. From their barracks in the old schloss park, the local Hitler Youth was discovered to be plotting to blow up the schloss with the civilian prisoners inside it! The internees worried desperately (as did prisoners-of-war) about what could be their fate. Would the German authorities decide to treat them as hostages and move them further behind the front line? Would the town of Wurzach be defended, in which case they were as much at risk of casualties as the local civilians? And would the Allied troops, when they arrived, recognise them as British or shoot first and ask questions later?

For days before their liberation, the internees could hear the sound of gunfire and see columns of smoke rising in the distance. They were confined inside the schloss but had a good view from the windows of

12. Idyll on the River Ach; Gloria's father considered this Wurzach scene
to be among his best paintings.

the chaos outside, as soldiers and civilians retreated through the town.
In one of his notes written later on the back of a painting, Thomas
Webber tells us something about what happened. This painting is a
front view of the schloss showing the pediment at roof level decorated
with a round mosaic of the figure of Christ put up by the Salvatorians
(see the front cover of this book). Thomas tells us that in the final days
of internment he watched from behind this pediment for the Allied
troops to arrive. His job was to tell the German camp commandant, so
that he would have time to show a Union Jack flag (painted on a bed
sheet), and alert the liberating troops to the nationality of the schloss
occupants.

In the event Wurzach was taken without a shot being fired after
local people removed the tank traps from the road to indicate that the
town would not be defended. This was in stark contrast to the village
of Ziegelbach, just five minutes up the road, which suffered badly from
shelling in a fierce firefight. Soon after midday on Saturday 28 April
1945, the first French tank arrived outside the schloss where its crew

broke through the barbed wire and were amazed to find themselves surrounded by hundreds of British civilians. They had no idea that these civilians would be there. The German commandant and guards had done their best for the internees right up until the end, remaining in post to protect them from diehards and hand them over safely. In return the internees now put in a good word for their captors; otherwise there was a risk they might be summarily shot.

The now ex-internees were initially granted freedom of movement and the Webber family decided to celebrate their liberation by taking a walk in the countryside. It turned out to be not such a good decision, as the French troops were still mopping up the resistance in the area. The family soon heard the sound of bullets whistling overhead and were forced to shelter in a ditch. They had to wait for things to calm down and then hurry back to the schloss. A new order was given confining everyone to camp, but this time for their safety.

13. A vibrant view of Wurzach painted by Gloria's father, with the fifteenth-century town hall (Rathaus) on the left.

The next few weeks were frustrating for the Jersey islanders as they waited to be repatriated and chafed at the delays. Dating from this time there is a photo of the Webber children together with the Paddock children, who occupied the next door room (illustration 1). The problem was where to send the ex-internees. The island of Jersey was not liberated until nearly two weeks after Wurzach, on 9

14. The interior of St Verena church in Wurzach by Thomas Webber.

May 1945, when the German garrison surrendered. But the Jersey economy was in ruins and the population starving, so they could not be sent back there. Eventually the decision was taken to fly them on Dakota aircraft to Hendon airport in the UK. The group was allocated places alphabetically so the Webbers were among the last to go, arriving in Hendon on 8 June 1945. After arrival procedures they went to live temporarily with Gloria's grandfather (on her father's side) in Abthorpe, Northamptonshire. There was no counselling or assistance available as there would be today. For some of the youngest children it was a shock to be suddenly transported out of the only world they knew, living cheek by jowl with hundreds of people.

In August 1945, as soon as the British government gave permission for the ex-internees to return home, Gloria and her family boarded the boat from Southampton to Jersey to pick up the pieces of their lives. They counted themselves fortunate because they were able to go back to their home in the village of Gorey, on the east coast of the island, which was still lived in by Gloria's grandmother and aunt (Elsie Webber's mother and sister). Many other internees had lost their homes on the island during their internment.

After leaving school Gloria worked in the famous Jersey Pottery which was established on the island in 1946. She moved to Cornwall with her husband after their marriage in 1954. Norman was a Cornishman and met Gloria when he visited Jersey to see relatives who lived there. Their first home in Cornwall was in St Austell where Norman worked in the China Clay industry. Later they moved to St Mawes and set up a haulage business. Gloria is a widow now; she still lives in St Mawes, which is where I met her and learned about her story.

15. Home on Jersey;
Gloria as a young woman.

21

5

RETURN
TO WURZACH

Twenty-five years after she left, in 1970, Gloria returned to Wurzach for the first time, together with her parents. They went as part of an organised group from Jersey to mark the twenty-fifth anniversary of the liberation of the internees. Gloria has very touching photos from this visit, showing the family outside the schloss. But, with hindsight she feels this return was far too soon and the visit not entirely a success. Not enough water had yet flowed under the bridge. When they arrived in Wurzach, Gloria's parents were apprehensive and reluctant to get off the coach. It took several minutes of coaxing from the local priest to persuade them that nothing awful was going to happen.

The process of recovery and reconciliation was extremely difficult for many of the ex-internees. Twelve of them died in Schloss Wurzach and are buried in the town cemetery. Many others suffered fractured lives. They have never received any compensation for their ordeal. From that 1970 return visit however, links began gradually to develop between Bad Wurzach (the town became a Spa town and gained the prefix Bad in 1950) and St Helier (the capital of Jersey). The path was slow and difficult, because of the residual pain and bitterness felt in Jersey over the occupation and deportations. Some ex-internees never wanted to be reminded of these years or to go back to where they were forcibly held. But eventually, in 2002, the towns were formally twinned showing there could be friendship between former enemies. Gloria's nephew (Clive Armstrong) is chairman of the twinning association.

16. Back at the camp – Gloria and her mother on the first return visit in 1970. The two windows of their room are marked by crosses on the photo.

Gloria returned to Wurzach for a second time in April 2005, on the sixtieth anniversary of the liberation. This visit was easier for her. As well as ex-internees, the group from Jersey included younger family members who did not share the same difficult history. The schloss had changed a great deal too and was home again (as it had been in the 1920s) to a secondary school. The school children put on a play for the returning internees and asked them to share their memories, as part of ensuring that nothing similar could ever happen again. There are happy photos from this visit including one of Gloria taken on *Marble Arch* (illustration 8), the magnificent staircase of Schloss Wurzach.

The final official return visit from Jersey to Wurzach took place between 25 and 29 April 2015, to celebrate seventy years since the schloss was liberated. Thirteen former internees, including Gloria, were among the group that made the trip. With the youngest of the surviving ex-internees now in their seventies and eighties, it was likely to be the last time most would go back to where they spent part of their childhood.

The visit included an official dinner in the schloss when internees spoke movingly about their incarceration as children, saying they had never experienced any cruelty from their captors and enjoyed so much kindness from the people of Bad Wurzach since. A tour of the building which had been their internment camp brought back poignant memories. In a ceremony at the war memorial in Bad Wurzach cemetery, a wreath of Jersey flowers was laid in memory of the twelve

17. Return to Wurzach: a group of ex-internees outside the schloss. Gloria is in the front row, second from the right.

18. Thomas Webber at the schloss in 1970.

islanders (men, women, and children) who died far from home and are buried here. Their names are listed on the war memorial alongside the German dead. In the park behind the schloss, where the Hitler Youth barracks had once been, a new statue was unveiled in honour of displaced people everywhere. And, most memorably, the ex-internees recreated their *Walk to Freedom* from the schloss on that day seventy years before when the Free French troops arrived. Newspapers in both Germany and Jersey carried photographs of Gloria and her childhood companions as they walked out of the main door of the schloss, not to meet French soldiers this time, but to be surrounded by cheering Bad Wurzach schoolchildren waving Jersey flags.

19. Schloss Wurzach by Thomas Webber.

20. Gloria and Norman Bullen on their wedding day.

One of Thomas Webber's most moving artworks is an illustrated poem about the invasion of Jersey and the deportation of the islanders. In the last verse of this poem he wrote,

> Now throughout the world we long to see
> The day of reckoning, for us Victory
> With Justice and Time and the Angel of Peace
> We pray thee God for hostilities to cease

MAP OF KEY LOCATIONS

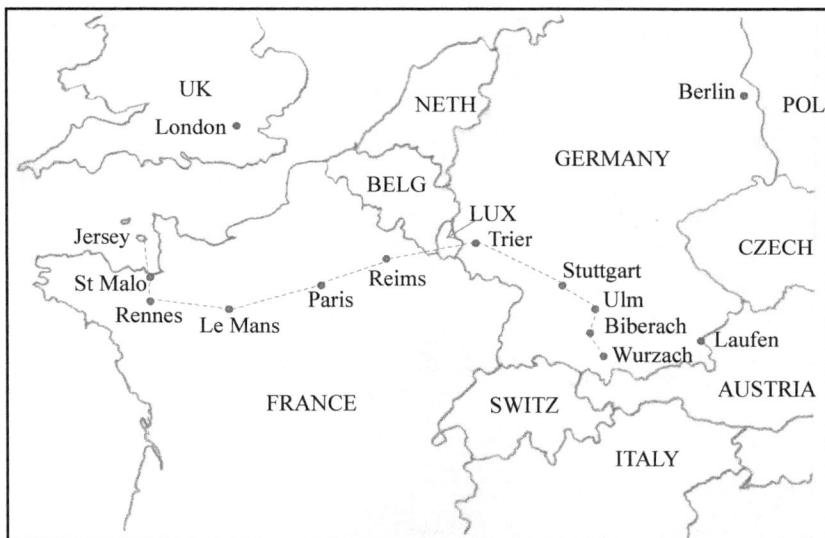

This hand-drawn map shows the location of Schloss Wurzach in south Germany and the route travelled by Gloria and her family on deportation from Jersey to internment in the schloss. It also shows the location of Schloss Laufen where the single men deported from Jersey were sent.

SOURCES

Recollections and personal archive of Mrs Gloria Bullen (born Webber)

Gisela Rothenhäusler. *Reaching across the Barbed Wire: French PoWs, Internees from the Channel Islands and Jewish Prisoners from Bergen-Belsen in Schloss Wurzach, 1940-1945).* Lindenberg: Kunstverlag Josef Fink, Jersey: Channel Islands Publishing. 2012.

Gillian Carr. *Occupied Behind Barbed Wire.* Jersey: Jersey Heritage Trust. 2009.

Roger E Harris. *Islanders Deported: Part 1: The complete history of those British subjects who were deported from the Channel Islands during the German Occupation of 1940-1945 and imprisoned in Europe.* Ilford, Essex: CISS Publishing. 1980.

Mrs G. Luce de Pre. *An Occupation Dairy: As published monthly in 'The Pilot', 1972-1973.* Transcribed by Tony Bellows.

S.P. Mackenzie. *The Colditz Myth: British and Commonwealth Prisoners of War in Nazi Germany.* Oxford: Oxford University Press. 2004.

Otto Frisch and Heinrich Fink. *Bad Wurzach: Seine Gemeinden und das Ried.* Bad Wurzach: Wurzach Verlag. 1991.

BOOKS IN THE SCHLOSS SERIES

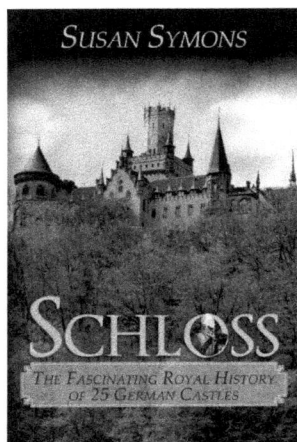

Schloss is the German word for castle or palace, and you are never far from one of these in Germany. For most of its history Germany was not a single country but a patchwork of royal states, held together under the banner of the Holy Roman Empire. The dukes and princes who ruled these states were passionate builders. Their beautiful castles and palaces, and their compelling personal stories, provide the material for the *Schloss* books.

This book can be seen as an inspiration ... to get out there and find the lesser known palaces and learn more about their history.
Royalty Digest Quarterly Journal

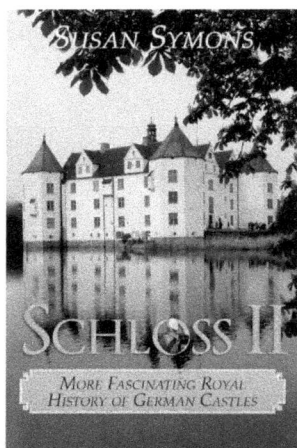

Each of these four *Schloss* books visits 25 beautiful castles and palaces in Germany and tells the colourful stories of the royal families that built and lived in them. Royalty have always been the celebrities of their day, and these stories from history can rival anything in modern-day television soap operas. The books are illustrated throughout and should appeal to anyone who likes history or sightseeing or is interested in people's personal stories.

The second volume is as good as the first, maybe even better – a must ...
Amazon review

FASCINATING ROYAL HISTORY

The stories in the *Schloss* books include the mistress of the king who tried to blackmail him and was imprisoned for forty-nine years; the princess from a tiny German state who used her body and her brains to become the ruler of the vast Russian empire; the prince who defied his family to marry a pharmacist's daughter and then bought her the rank of royal princess; and the duke whose personal story is so colourful he has been called the Bavarian Henry VIII!

Susan Symons has done another fantastic job, proving the point that history can also be fun ...
The European Royal History Journal

The German princes abdicated in 1918, at the end of World War I, and Germany became a republic. As they lost their royal families, many of the castles and palaces went into decline and became prisons, workhouses, and other institutions. Some were behind the Iron Curtain for fifty years. The books chart these difficult years and their resurgence and use today as public buildings, museums, and hotels.

If you thought history was dull, this author will make you think again.
Roseland Festival

www.ingramcontent.com/pod-product-compliance
Lightning Source LLC
Chambersburg PA
CBHW071653040426
42452CB00009B/1856